I WANT TO KNOW ABOUT

WHICH IS THE BIGGEST ANIMAL BABY IN THE WORLD ?

and other questions about baby animals

Compiled by :
Meesha Khanna

Illustrated by :
Kiran, Mohan & Dayal

Published by

DREAMLAND PUBLICATIONS

J-128, KIRTI NAGAR, NEW DELHI - 110 015 (INDIA)
Tel : 011-2510 6050 Fax : 011-2543 8283
E-mail : dreamland@vsnl.com
www.dreamlandpublications.com

Published in 2008 by
DREAMLAND PUBLICATIONS
J-128, Kirti Nagar, New Delhi - 110 015 (India)
Tel : 011-2510 6050, Fax : 011-2543 8283
E-mail : dreamland@vsnl.com, www.dreamlandpublications.com

ISBN 978-81-8451-029-4

Printed by

EIH LIMITED

A member of The Oberoi Group
UNIT PRINTING PRESS

PREFACE

'I Want To Know About' series provides young children with an excellent starting-point for exploring different topics. It is designed to capture the imagination of the children and arouse their curiosity to know more about many fascinating facts. It is a fun-filled, entertaining book. It also answers demanding questions in a child-friendly and informative style.

The entire series is the result of well-integrated efforts of the entire team of Dreamland. It is hoped that the intended purpose of this book meets the children's requirement.

—Publisher

CONTENTS

Who has got the best mother ?

A baby gorilla's mother grooms her baby, feeds it for upto three years and protects and helps it for longer still. Though she may look a bit frightening to us, but she's loving and caring to her young. So a baby gorilla has one of the best mother in the world.

● Along with chimpanzees, gibbons and orang-utans, gorillas are a type of ape. And not only gorillas all the apes make good mothers.

Who has got the worst mother ?

The female European cuckoo is a lazy mother who can't be bothered to look after her chicks. She even lays her egg in another bird's nest. It's the other bird that does all the hard work, when the egg hatches. She even raises the chick.

● Cuckoo's egg matches the other ones in the nest. So she manages to trick birds.

Whose babies are stuck inside the prison ?

The male hornbill helps the female to block up the door, while the female is laying her eggs in a hole in a tree. But for her beak he leaves a hole so that he can feed her while she's stuck inside !

● Tree shrews leave their babies in the nest, only popping by to feed them every other day. So they are part-time mothers.

Which male animal gives birth to his young?

There is a special pouch on the body of the male seahorse where the female lays her eggs. Till the time they hatch, the male has to carry them around. Hundreds of baby seahorses shoot out into the sea then.

Do you know whose feet keep an egg warm?

In the middle of winter every year, a female emperor peguin lays one egg and to keep it warm gives it to her mate. Until it hatches in early spring he balances the egg between his feet and his feathers.

● Most animal fathers leave their babies before they are even born. So they play no part in raising up their young ones.

The young ones of sticklebacks are looked after by the male sticklebacks. The father grabs the baby in his mouth and spits it back in the nest, if the baby tries to swim off.

Whose father has a chest like a sponge ?

In Africa, Asia and Southern Europe Sandgrouse live in the dry desert. The male flies hundreds of kilometres to a water hole, when water's short and soaks up water in his feathers. For a long refreshing drink, he then flies back to his thirsty chicks and lets them suck out the water.

Do you know why kangaroos have pouches?

For the growth of a baby a pouch is a safe place. When a kangaroo is born, its size is only the size of a peanut. Until it reaches the pouch, it struggles through its mum's fur. There, it carries on growing by feeding on her milk.

● The males don't have babies so they don't need a pouch. So only female kangaroos have one.

● Taking care not to bite the babies with her razor-sharp teeth, a female crocodiles bears them in her mouth.

Who takes a ride on the water ?

Baby grebes are perfectly able to swim on their own but they often like to ride along on their mother's back

Who rides on its mum's back ?

For the first seven months of its life a baby lemur rides on its mother's back. By wraping its legs around her, the baby holds on tightly as the mother leaps through the forest on a hair raising ride.

Who's lifted by the scruff of the neck ?

A leopard lifts her cub by gripping the back of its neck in her mouth, like all cat mothers. The cub isn't hurt, as the skin is very loose and baggy here. Until she gently puts it down again, it hangs quite still.

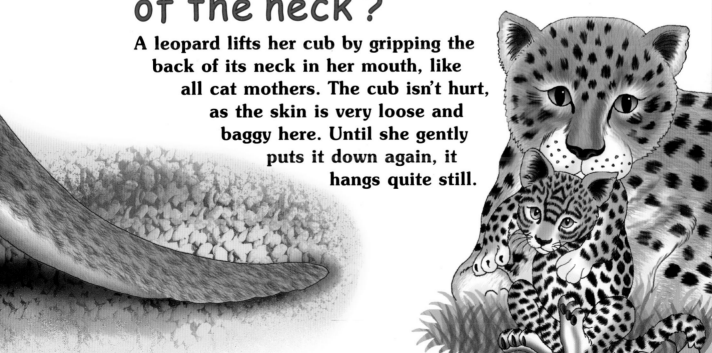

Do you know which baby has lots of cousins?

A baby elephant has a large number of aunt's, grannies, sisters and cousins inspite of having a mother. Due to the reason that female elephants live in large family groups of up to 50 animals.

● A hippo mother leaves her calf with a baby-sitter, when she goes off to feed.

Do you know whose babies stay in a nursery?

To make sure that babies aren't lonely, mara parents leave them underground with lots of families sharing the same burrow. A mother checks up on the other mara babies too when she drops by to feed her young.

● Maras are a kind of long-legged guinea pig who live in South America. Mara parents by no means stay with their babies in the burrow. They whistle down the hole and the young approach dashing out.

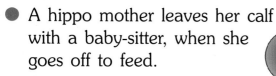

Do you know which is the biggest nursery?

In the United States, Bracken Cave is home to over twenty million bats. Huddled together for warmth, the mothers leave their babies in a nursery. The bats are so closely packed, there may be a thousand in a space the size of a doormat.

- Bees eggs hatch out in a special part of the hive. So they use nurseries too.

- A bat mother recognises her baby's call from millions of others in the cave, as she has got such sharp hearing.

11

What do you find inside a bird's egg?

A birds egg contains three things — a baby bird, a yellow yolk and a clear jelly named the white. The food for the growing bird is the yolk. The white protects the bird if the egg gets a knock, but it is also the food.

● Though sharks are the size of a rugby ball but they lay the biggest eggs.

What makes birds turn their eggs?

To give every part of the egg its fair share of warmth, birds turn their eggs. A parent has to sit on the nest because the baby birds need warmth to grow.

- A kiwi chick takes three months or more to hatch but a baby housefly takes just 24 hours. So some eggs take less time and some more to hatch.

- Some eggs are eaten by hungry hunters. So they don't get the chance to hatch.

Do only birds lay eggs?

Not only birds but all sorts of animals like frogs, fish, turtles, snakes, spiders, insects lay eggs. Though the look and feel of all the eggs are different. Butterfly eggs are tiny and often shine like shiny jewels. Turtle eggs are soft and leathery and the size of golf balls.

- Caterpillars gobble up their eggshells as they hatch. So they seem to be born hungry.

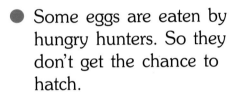
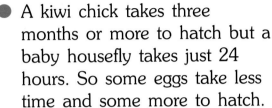

Do you know which baby lives in a comfiest nest ?

Baby rabbits mother builds the nest inside a burrow putting dry grass stalks into a cushion, and then covering it with her own soft fur. So they have a nest that is very cosy.

● A baby pack rat's nest is build in a prickly cactus. So it isn't lucky as a baby rabbit.

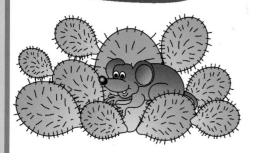

Whose baby is born under the snow ?

Polar bear's mother digs an underground den, deep in the snow where it's baby is born. Making the den a snug place to spend the winter months, warm air is trapped inside it.

Do you know which nests are 100 years old?

Year after year American bald eagles fly back to the same nest. They lay their eggs after making a few repairs. The age of some nests is over 100 years, and are heavier and bigger than a car.

● The size of a hummingbird's nest is about the size of a walnut. Spider's silk, lichen, flower petals and plant fluff is used to make it.

● A pair of woodpeckers build their nest in the space shuttle in the United States. Though they didn't blast off with it.

Who makes a bubbly froth?

Baby froghoppers make a bubbly froth very soon after they're born so they are often known as spittlebags. While they feed and grow, they hide in this 'Cuckoo spit'.

Which is the biggest animal baby in the world?

Weighing as much as 1,000 human babies that is up to 3,000 kilograms, the baby blue whale is a real whopper. Its mother takes it to the bottom to take a first breath of air, as soon as it is born.

The height of baby blue whale is as long as five scuba divers swimming tip to toe.

Do you know who is the tallest baby ?

Taller than most grown-up people, a baby giraffe is about two metres tall. The mother giraffe's baby hits the ground feet first as the mother giraffe is very tall and gives birth standing up.

- The baby howler monkey's cries can be heard even through thick rainforest. So it is a champion screamer.

- One of the dangerous babies would be the young dragonfly. It has got spiky jaws with which it dutches almost anything in rivers and lakes.

Who has got the ugliest baby ?

The vulture chick is one of the ugliest looking babies, with its bare head and neck and big hooked beak. But not only the baby, its parents are also very ugly. Maybe it's because of eating all the rotting meat.

Do you know why pandas have one baby at a time?

A mother giant panda can only cope with one cub at a time as she gives it so much love and attention. She is helping to make sure that her baby survives, by looking after her cub for a year or more.

● Zookeepers send their pandas around the world so they can meet other pandas and hopefully have babies. As there aren't many pandas left.

Who has four indentical babies?

A nine-banded armadillo has four identical babies, each time it gives birth. All are either male or female. This happens because inside the mother a single egg splits into four, and all four parts start their growth into identical quadruplets !

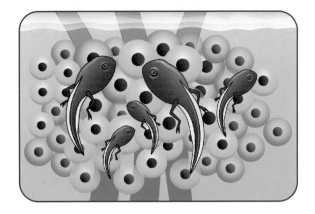

Who lay hundreds of eggs ?

In a big frothy mass called spawn, most frogs and toads lay hundreds of eggs. Only some of the eggs survive and hatch into tadpoles as most of them are eaten.

- In every two years only one egg is layed by the Albatross mother. Until the chic is big enough to fly it is looked after by its parents for about ten months.

- Every year the female giant clam lays at least a billion of eggs so it may have the biggest family of all.

Do you know which baby gets the creamiest milk?

A mother harp seal's milk is about 12 time creamier than cow's milk. It is so thick and rich that it looks more like mayonnaise than milk. The harp seal pup can be seen almost growing fatter when it feeds as it is such good food.

● A large number of seal pups are born in the coldest parts of the world. But as they have a thick layer of fat covered by a furry coat to keep them nice and warm, they don't freeze to death.

● A seal pup has to develop speedily so that its mother can go off and catch fish. She spends three weeks just giving food to her pup— after that she's hungry.

Do you know which parent serves meals in a bag?

There is a baggy pouch of skin under the pelican's beak. It uses it to carry fish. By draining the water it swallows them all. The parent brings up a mouthful of fish and lets the baby feed from the pouch when a chick needs feeding.

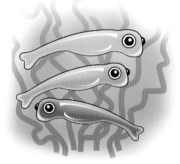

● A baby salmon has a pouch of food rather like an egg yolk, that keeps it going for several weeks. So the tiny fish hatches with its own packed lunch.

● One of the hungriest babies must be the polyphemus moth caterpillar. It eats 86,000 times its own birth-weight in leaves, in the first 56 days of its life.

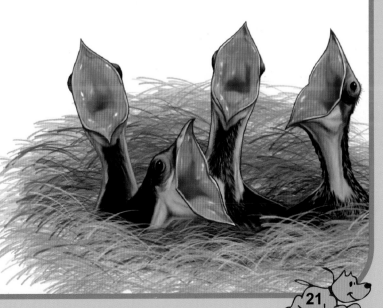

● The insides of the mouth of many baby birds are brightly coloured. According to some people this encourages the parents to feed the hungry chicks.

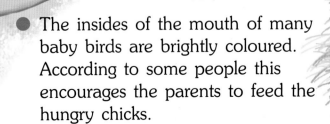

What makes lion cubs follow their mother's tail?

Lion cubs are very mischievous, and jump on anything that moves – specially the tassel on the end of their mother's tail. Games like this, train the cubs how to follow and attack suddenly — talents they'll require when they have to hunt for themselves.

● The mother of the sea otters tosses her baby into the air, and then catches it again. So they know how to have fun.

● Play is how baby animals learn all kinds of essential skills for grown-up life.

● The mother of bear cubs teach them how to catch fish. With their paws they scoop them out of the river.

● Baby chimps soon learn how to dig for termites with a stick as few parents teach their young how to use tools.

How do ducklings play follow-my-leader ?

Ducklings follow the first moving thing they see when they hatch, which is normally their mother. They learn how to swim and feed, by following her everywhere. She only has to call and they fall in line, if they wander off !

How does a puppy change into a dog?

At the time of birth each puppy is blind and helpless but it will be fully grown by the time it's two years old. Whatever type of dog they are all pups are roughly the same size when they're born. So to finish growing up it takes smaller breeds less time !

2. The puppy is starting to explore, by six weeks. It enjoys playing with its sisters and brothers.

1. After about two weeks a puppy will start walking. As after that time it's eyes and ears open.

● Before starting walking, a baby wildebeest runs ! Just five minutes after the youngster is born, it trots.

3. The dog is strong and active by the time it is fully grown. To stay fit, good food and exercise will help it.

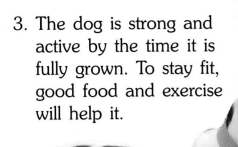

Do you know when does a tiger cub leave home?

Until the cubs are about two years old, a mother tiger looks after them. But after they are two-year-olds she starts ignoring them. She thinks that they are grown up and should start looking after themselves.

Larva

Pupa

● Most insects while growing, change shape. As a wriggly larva, a beetle starts life. It then becomes a pupa. Inside the hard skin the insect is changing fast, though it may not look like it's doing much. It's a fully-grown beetle when it crawls out.

Beetle

Who hides in the forest after sensing danger ?

A fawn, which is a young deer is very wobbly on its legs. It couldn't excape from a hungry cougar or wolf. The young animal freezes and remains completely still until the danger has passed. The fawn has a speckled coat which helps it seem almost invisible in the forest's dappled light.

Do you know which babies hide in a circle of horns ?

When danger threatens, adult musk oxen makes a circle around their calves with their heads lowered, they stand close together infront of the enemy like a row of shields. To attack the wall of long, curved horns, it takes a brave and hungry wolf to attack !

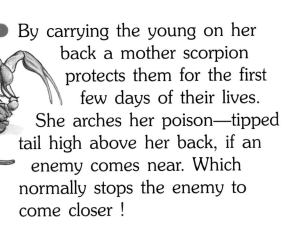

● By carrying the young on her back a mother scorpion protects them for the first few days of their lives. She arches her poison—tipped tail high above her back, if an enemy comes near. Which normally stops the enemy to come closer !

● To scare away enemies, lots of animals make noises. Young burrowing owls can make a noise like a rattlesnake which live in holes in the ground when they are threatened.

Who's mother pretends she's sick ?

The mother bird acts as if she is wounded, if a hungry hunter threatens a plover's nest. As if the wings is broken, she flaps it and flutters weakly along the ground, going away from the nest. To protect her babies, she wants her enemy to think that she is injured and would be easy to capture. So that leaving her babies, the enemy would go after her.

Which mother always washes her baby

From the moment the kittens are born, a mother cat starts licking them. To keep the kitten warm, the mother's tongue dries the kitten's fur. Licking roughly around the new-born kitten's mouth makes it gasp and start breathing too.

● A foal sometimes acts friendly with its mother by biting it. This is its way of asking its mother to groom its coat.

● Flamingos chick's feathers as well as their own are preened by them. They spread oil over the feathers after pecking out dirt and insects. This oil which comes from the bird's oil glands makes the feathers waterproof.

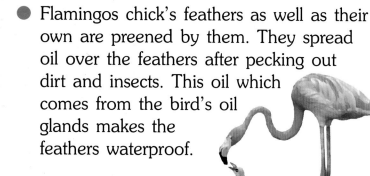

Who's babies are well groomed ?

A baboon babies enjoys a good groom. The mother working slowly, section by section, parts the baby's fur and picks dirt carefully with her fingers. She removes dirt, insects and pieces of dead skin. Not only this she eats most of her findings.

You might not like to clean yourself with mud but a baby hippo likes nothing more than a mudbath. This is because the mud keeps the hippo's skin soft by protecting it from the sun.

Do you know who's baby lives in the cleanest nest ?

Though several animals keep their babies nest clean, but the badger would take the first position in this task. By regularly lining their burrows with fresh dried grass and leaves, the adult badgers even dig special holes well away from the burrow. These holes are used as toilets by the whole family.

Do you know how a lamb find its mother ?

Sometimes in a crowded field, mother sheep and their lambs get separated. Each lamb has its own distinctive call, though most of them look similar. Every mother sheep can easily find its baby in the crowd as she knows its baby's cry.

● Using clicks and other sounds, several whales and dolphins talk to their young. A baby humpback can never gets lost as it can hear its mother from up to 185 km.

● A baby moose is nudged by its mother from behind. This is the way of telling the mother to the baby that it has to keep moving on, even if it is feeling tired !

Who's baby gets smacked when its naughty ?

The mother of baby elephant punishes her calf by whacking it with her trunk when its naughty. This way the calf learns how to behave. But the mother elephant also knows to show affection. She uses her trunk to store her baby and other young elephants in the herd.

● By copying the sounds of their parents the wolf cubs learn to howl.

● To prevent the young from floating away in the current, the manatee nuzzles her young and cradles it in her flippers.

Index

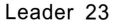